PATRICIA D. WRIGHT

NURSING SURVIVAL GUIDE

What They Don't Teach You in Nursing School

Nursing Survival Guide

Copyright 2019 by Patricia Diane Wright

Unless otherwise noted, scriptures are taken from The Holy Bible New Kings James Version

Copyright 1982 by Thomas Nelson, Inc.
Used by permission.

Printed in the United States of America
ISBN: 9798643524083

Nursing Survival Guide
TABLE OF CONTENTS

WHAT THEY DON'T TEACH YOU IN NURSING SCHOOL

When I started as a nurse almost 25 years ago, I felt like nursing school did not prepare me for the emotional rollercoaster I would face as a nurse. So, I took the information I learned over the years that I had applied to my own life to help me deal with the stress and prevent burn out that being a nurse can cause. Most of us started as a nurse because we found enjoyment in helping others. It wasn't for the money but it was because we have a servant's heart.

And let us not grow weary while doing good, for in due season we shall reap if we do not lose heart (Galatians 6:9)

This scripture serves as a reminder when you're having a hard day at work, your behind in your med pass, because you had 2 admits, patient just fell, all while you have a patient actively dying. Don't grow weary, step back take a deep breath, and say, "God I'm doing this for you."

I'm not going to sugar coat it for you rookie nurses. I'm here to tell you sometimes your job as a nurse can be so overwhelming it will cause you to cry and even feel like quitting. When I get that stressed at work, I do as it says in these scriptures, I cry out.

From the end of the earth I will cry to you. When my heart is overwhelmed: Lead me to the rock that is higher than I. (Psalms 61:2)

In my distress I cried to the Lord, And He heard me. (Psalms 120:1)

Believe me when I say this, as my coworkers can attest, I say aloud when I am really overwhelmed "Help me Lord Help me". It helps calm me, reducing my anxiety to get through those rough moments. It must work because my staff tells me, "your always calm when it gets crazy".

I have come to realize, God and I are in this together, we are a team, he is my rock. It's kind of like that credit card commercial that says "don't leave home without it". Well I'm here to tell you that as a nurse you can't leave home without God when you go to work. God has you as long as you continue doing good for others and not let yourself grow weary and get burned out. Even God took a day to rest. It's ok to take time for yourself, it's not selfish. How can you care for others if your run down? Here is a worldly example for you people who fly. On a plane, they tell you in their safety briefing before the plane takes off that if the oxygen masks drop from the ceiling put the oxygen mask on yourself first before helping others with theirs. Yes, you won't be much help if your passed out from lack of oxygen. I know we have a tendency as nurses to put our patient's wellbeing first but we have to take care of ourselves as well. So, take that bathroom break and take time to eat.

If you do it Gods way it won't go unnoticed. It will result in favor, promotions, pay raises and bonuses. I am an LPN, but this did not stop Gods advancement for me. He opened doors for me to work in other positions as a nurse. I worked as a Wound Nurse, as the Staff Development Coordinator and as the Restorative Program Coordinator.

It's amazing what positions will open up when you do it Gods way. It even allowed me to train employees whom had more credentials than I did. This brings me to another scripture, *if they obey and serve Him, they shall spend their days in prosperity and their years in pleasures. (Job 36:11)*

But he who looks into the perfect law of liberty and continues in it, and is not a forgetful hearer but a doer of the work, this one will be blessed in what he does. (James 1:25)

"Let your light so shine before men, that they may see your good works and glorify your Father in heaven (Matthew 5:16)

You have a heart to serve others. Doesn't it bring you joy when you made a positive impact on someone's life or you see miracles of healing take place in one of your patients? It's amazing what can happen when you allow God to work through you.

And we know that all things work together for good to those who love God, to those who are the called according to His purpose (Romans 8:28)

How can you go wrong caring for others if you're doing God's work? His purpose is being done through you. He is working in you and through you to help heal people.

So, I'm sure you're asking, "how do I do it Gods way?" Well glad you asked, let me tell you.

HOW TO DO GODS WORK AS A NURSE

START WITH PRAYER. Every day on my way to work, I pray: Lord, work through me and guide my steps to help me do my job safely and effectively, help me to be a blessing to my patients and my coworkers, help me to accept the things I have no control over and give me the courage to change the things I can through prayer, words and laying of hands. Help me to be the light you shine through to represent you, Amen

"And whatever things you ask in prayer, believing, you will receive." (Matthew 21:22)

Evening and morning and at noon I will pray, and cry aloud, and He shall hear my voice. (Psalm 55:17)

"Praying always with all prayer and supplication in the spirit, being watchful to this end with all perseverance and supplication for all saints (Ephesians 6:18)

LEARN TO LISTEN

It's amazing when you bring God to work with you, he will guide your work, if you're willing to listen.

A wise man will hear and increase learning, and a man of understanding will attain wise counsel (Proverbs 1:5)

Incline your ear and hear the words of the wise, and apply your heart to my knowledge; (Proverbs 22:17)

God is the all-knowing he sees what you don't. The Bible even tells you *I will instruct you and teach you in the way you should go; I will guide you with my eye. (Psalm 32:8)*

Don't be in such a hurry that you may miss his voice or his wise counsel. Do you think God hurried things? All things are done in their right time. Your goal should be to get your job done in a safe manner and not on how quick you can do it.

For example: You're sitting at your desk charting and that still small voice in your head saying, check on so and so patient. You are really trying to get out on time and finish your shift, but don't ignore that voice. I know from experience when you ignore the voice, nothing good comes from it.

He who heeds the word wisely will find good, and whoever trusts the Lord happy is he (Proverbs 16:20)

So, you then listen to the voice and you go to the patient's room to find that patient potentially in harm's way by almost falling out of bed or has his or her IV halfway pulled out. Even that voice that says, check those meds one more time before giving them to the patient. Learn to trust that still small voice, it's there to protect you and your patient. Remember who you really work for, God. It's like if your earthly boss tells you to go do something, typically speaking you would go do it, right. Same with God if he is telling you in that small voice to go check on that patient or check those meds one more time, just do it because it will work out in your favor.

YOU'RE NOT ALONE

If God is going to be effective in working through you to help others, you have to bring him to work with you.

For I, the Lord your God, will hold your right hand, saying to you, "Fear not, I will help you." (Isaiah 41:13)

So, we boldly say: "the Lord is my helper; I will not fear. What can man do to me?" (Hebrews 13:6)

God is your helper and he is the all-knowing. The Bible is an amazing guide to tell you how to live the right way, but you have to follow the word for it to work for your good. When doing God's work, healing people is not always easy. So, it's good to get wise counsel. Like in the Bible when Moses father-in-law says these words to Moses "both you and these people who are with you will surely wear yourselves out, for this thing is too much for you; you are not able to perform it by yourself. "Listen to my voice; I will give you counsel, and God will be with you: stand before God for the people, so that you may bring the difficulties to God (Exodus 18:18-19)

God knows the challenges you will face as a nurse and he knows how hard it will be at times. God works through people to heal others. Just like he used his disciples Peter and Paul; in which is demonstrated in couple different ways: through words, touch and presence.

Where Peter sees a lame man lying outside the temple and Peter said "Silver and gold I do not have, but what I do have I give you: In the name of Jesus Christ of Nazareth, rise up and walk." (Acts 3:6-7)

Peter had the power of God inside of him and delivered it through his words. Words have power and Yes you can heal people with your words just as easily as you can tear someone down with words.

In Acts 20:7-12 a man had fallen out of a third story window and died; yet Paul wrapped his arms around the dead body and said "he's alive" through Paul's touch and words this man was healed. I had this happen to a patient of mine. She fell down a flight of stairs, had a head injury, had a Tracheostomy to breath and was fed via a tube and couldn't walk. Because a nurse had the courage to use words to speak life and to lay hands on this patient. This patient was healed and restored; she had her feeding tube removed and was able to eat on her own, she had her tracheostomy device removed and was able to breath on her own. This patient was able to walk out of the health care facility restored and healed. The care staff can attest that she had an overnight healing. God is Amazing.

Another example of healing is mentioned in Acts 5:12-16 where the shadow of Peter would cause the sick to be healed. Can you imagine being so full of God that his light shines through you, that even your shadow can heal people?

Have you ever wondered that maybe God is waiting for you to allow him in your life so he can work in you and though you on this level?

I would love for God to use me this way, because it would make being a nurse a whole lot easier. Imagine for a moment that just your presence could heal people.

Of course, I couldn't get away with writing this guide without including Jesus way of healing. During the time Jesus was alive he healed multitudes of people with just his presence which was referenced in Matthew 4:24, Matthew 9:21, Matthew 9:35, Matthew 14:14, Matthew 14:36, Matthew 15:30, Mark 1:34. Mark 3:10, Mark 6:56, Luke 6:18, Luke 7:21 and Luke 9:11. He healed the lame, the blind, the mute, epileptic, the paralyzed, diseased, tormented, evil spirited and demon possessed people with his *presence*. You have been commissioned, given the authority and power to go and do the same. Jesus told us this for obvious reasons, because he cannot be here to heal the sick personally. Yet he needs you to allow him to work through you to be able to heal people.

Then Jesus shows us another example on how to heal in Matthew 8:16 where he cast out spirits and demons with *a word*. Just another example of how words heal people. Wouldn't this be great for our ever-growing psych patient population. It saddens me to see how these people are tormented and we as nurses hold superpowers (words) within us to set them free and heal them. The third way Jesus shows us how to heal people, is laying of hands.

When the sun was setting, all those who had Any that were sick with various diseases brought them to Him; and He laid His hands on every one of them and healed them. (Luke 4:40)

Now He could do no mighty work there, except that He laid hands on a few sick people and healed them. And he marveled because of their unbelief. Then he went about the village in a circuit teaching. (Mark 6:5-6)

This verse brings up a great point; you're going to run across people who don't want to be healed for whatever reason. I have experienced that as well. The best thing to do when this happens is to take it to God and pray that they have a change of heart. Don't let their unbelief steal your joy.

"These things I have spoken to you, that My joy may remain in you, and that your joy may be full. (John 15:11)

GOOD TIME MANAGEMENT

He who keeps his command will experience nothing harmful; and a wise man's heart discerns both time and judgement (Ecclesiastes 8:5)

Working as a nurse there are times you don't get breaks because of incidents that are out of your control. But what about the times you do get a break or a little down time. How are you using this time? Are you using it playing candy crush, taking a smoke break or gossiping?

How could you use that time more productively?

Or what about the times that you're not on break but your giving patient care or doing a med pass and you just can't seem to get it done in a timely manner. Something that works for me is on the drive home I evaluate how my day went and think of ways I can make the next day at work better.

I think of ways to improve my time and to improve the care I give. I then take about 5 minutes to write these things down when I get home. This helps in 2 ways: **1.** Helps me be prepared for tomorrow and start the work day with confidence **2.** It helps me to not spend the rest of my day focused on the bad day I had. By writing it down it gets it out of your mind so you can focus on your spouse, your children or even your hobbies.

This brings me to an Important point about using your time wisely; don't let your family suffer at the expense of your job. Yes, nurses work long hours, I so understand. But are you picking up extra hours to make more money while your health declines or your family suffers? I have seen this a lot with health care workers and experienced it myself. Before you pick up extra hours at work ask yourself a couple questions: Do I really need the extra money? Will this hinder my marriage? Will my children suffer from me not being home? I understand there are times when you need to make little extra cash for things that come up like home improvements or other things that are out of your control, but this should only be for a season, not forever.

If your putting all your time into your nursing work it will make you out of balance and other areas of your life will suffer. Even God took a day to rest.

DO IT WITHOUT COMPLAINING

Do all things without complaining and disputing, that you may become blameless and harmless, children of God without fault in the midst of a crooked and perverse generation, among whom you shine as light in the world. (Philippians 2:14-15)

Things are going to happen at work that may just tick you off, but is it really productive to complain about it? Here are a few irritating things that I have experienced during my time as a nurse: Your passing meds only to find that the 1st couple patients you have to pass meds to are out of what they need, or you need to get vitals on a patient, draw blood, start an IV or start a tube feeding and you don't have the supplies you need to do your job. Yes, I so have been there. This can surely add stress to anyone's day. On the brighter side it teaches you to be creative. Times like these you're going to save yourself time by not complaining, besides it's not going to change your situation. Instead of going to 5 people to complain about it, try going to the person whom can help you in that given situation.

Other times I have experienced people complaining is when they get mandated or work short staffed. Yes, this does happen to healthcare workers. You will have to do the best you can with what you got.

It's part of the business, because we can't just cancel work if there is not enough staff. These patients depend on us. Is it fair to the patient whom is sick, to hear staff complaining and pointing fingers of who is to blame? These patients have their own stress and here you come venting and complaining to them, in which is not going to help them heal. God is a great listener. Matter of fact if you vent to him, he could actually help you deal with these problems that arise that are out of your control.

TO BE A COMFORTER

= is to ease or alleviate a person's feelings of grief or distress

God is not only your comforter during your time of need but he works through you as a nurse to comfort others.

These verses mentioned below show us that.

"Comfort, yes, comfort My people!" says your God (Isaiah 40:1)

God is our strength in time of trouble, yet we need to be our patient's strength in their time of trouble it's a Co-laboring with God.

But the salvation of the righteous is from the Lord: He is their strength in the time of trouble. (Psalm 37:39)

Blessed be the God and Father of our Lord Jesus Christ, the Father of mercies and God of all comfort, who comforts us in all our tribulation, that we may be able to comfort those who are in any trouble, with the comfort with which we ourselves are comforted by God. (2 Corinthians 1:3-4)

As nurses we treat more than just the physical body of a person. We are treating the person as a whole. We treat their physical, spiritual, emotional, mental, social and financial well-being. If you just focus on the physical problem, you're doing your patient a disservice.

DEALING WITH DIFFICULT PATIENTS

When a man's ways please the Lord, He makes even his enemies to be at peace with him (Proverbs16:7)

Now we exhort you, brethren, warn those who are unruly, comfort the faint hearted, uphold the weak be patient with all. See that no one renders evil for evil to anyone, but always pursue what is good for yourselves and for all. (Thessalonians 5:14-15)

The Bible clearly states, BE PATIENT WITH ALL, yes even the unruly. I can so understand how hard it can be especially with the patient who put their call light on 100 times. Learn to be empathetic, maybe the individual is scared to be alone and doesn't know how to express it. Talk to them, try to get them to reveal why they keep acting in these difficult ways. Arguing with the patient will only make matters worse. You may even run across a patient whom hits or kicks you. In the passage above reminds us to not render evil for evil; which means don't treat them unkind in return. In times like these it will be beneficial to remember why you became a nurse in the first place. We all have a run in with difficult patients from time to time. I'm not telling you to allow them to hurt you; you need to protect yourself. But learn to cherish the good days and to not take these bad incidences personal. This brings me to another point, forgive them. Yes, I said it, FORGIVE THEM.

BE FORGIVING

When dealing with the difficult patients, for example your head injury patients, your psych patients or your patients with dementia it's good to remember these scriptures in the Bible where Jesus said *"Father, forgive them, for they do not know what they do." (Luke 23:34)*

And Jesus also said *"For if you forgive men their trespasses your Heavenly Father will also forgive you". (Matthew 6:14)*

We work in a profession where we deal with people. People can be unreasonable and self-centered. Some patients will totally understand what they are doing when they are being difficult. You're going to have indifferences, but you still have to forgive them. How can you do what you have been called to do "heal them", when you can't even forgive them? We are all a work in progress.

The Lord tells us *"if my people who are called by my name will humble themselves, and pray and seek my face, and turn from their wicked ways, then I will hear from heaven, and will forgive their sin and heal the land." (2 Chronicles 7:14)*

We need to look inside ourselves and ask what could I do different to help this situation. Believe me I have had times where I became short with a patient and had to apologize to God first for falling short and then go apologize to the patient with my tail between my legs. If you don't forgive the patient and yourself it leaves no room for God to work in you to heal his people, because you will be filled up with hatred and resentment. Besides un-forgiveness is like acid to your body, it will cause you to age quickly, and get burned out. It can also cause you to have physical ailments like pain and a decreased immune system making you more prone to getting sick. Working in the health field you can't afford to have a decreased immune system because you come in contact with anything and everything. Best words of advice I ever got was from my grandfather before he went to be with the Lord. When I went to visit him, I asked him, Pops what do I have to do to live to be as old as you? My grandfather replied with "forgive everyone, even if they have done you wrong and stay active". That was so profound I live by these words today.

Bearing with one another, and forgiving one another, if anyone has a complaint against another; even as Christ forgave you, so you also must do (Colossians 3:13)

TO BE AN ADVOCATE FOR YOUR PATIENT

Nursing school doesn't prepare you to deal with situations where you have to go against the grain. Sometimes decisions are made for the patient that are not the best for that individual. So, you have to be able to speak up for your patients so things can be done in their best interest, especially when they can't speak for themselves.

Let your speech always be with grace, seasoned with salt, that you may know how you ought to answer each one (Colossians 4:6)

You need to know how and when to stand up for what's right. There was one time I remembered when a doctor gave me a direct order and I knew it was wrong so I questioned him on it and he became angry with me and asked to speak with my supervisor. I stood my ground because what's wrong is wrong no matter who's doing it. Of course, I had to explain what happened to my boss and my boss agreed with me that the doctor was wrong. Sometimes doing the right thing is not the favorable thing to do. It may even make people mad at you, but if you know beyond a shadow of a doubt that you're doing the right thing and working in the patient's best interest. It will all work out for your good and the good of your patient if you do it Gods way.

Open your mouth for the speechless, in the cause of all who are appointed to die (Proverbs 31:8)

TO BE A PROTECTOR

"But whoever listens to me will dwell safely, and will be secure, without fear of evil" (Proverbs 1:33)

As a nurse you not only heal patients but you need to protect them from harm. Protect them by doing your job safely, protect them from hurting themselves or being hurt by others. There are different types of abuse that we need to protect them from: physical harm, neglect, sexual abuse, verbal and emotional abuse, financial abuse and discriminatory abuse.

This means we need to keep our eyes and ears open to be effective at preventing abuse from happening or responding quickly to abuse that occurred to get the individual out of harmful situation. One of the bigger challenges I find in nursing is that "patients have the right to fall". Yes, but we still have to protect them. So, nurses this is where the challenge lies: we have to get creative to come up with solutions to prevent them from getting injured when they fall. That's why is so important to listen to that small voice nudging you to go check on a patient, because it might be that nudge that gets you to stop what you're doing and go check on that patient preventing a fall. I have experienced it many times throughout my nursing career. Believe me that small voice or gut instinct some call it will save you and the patient every time.

TO BE COURAGEOUS

I can do all things through Christ who strengthens me (Philippians 4:13)

Wait on the Lord; Be of good courage, and he shall strengthen your heart; Wait, I say on the Lord (Psalms 27:14)

As a nurse you have to be clear in your own values and having the personal strength to take risks while doing what is right.

You will be presented with situations that you don't agree with and you will have one of two choices to make: **1.** Go with the flow and keep doing things as usual or **2.** Speak up to do the right thing and hold people accountable.

It takes courage to do some of the things we do as nurses. Here's an example that takes courage, used for dramatization: you have a patient whom comes into the ER after just killing a police officer and he codes and no one is jumping in to start CPR immediately, but you jump in and start it, why because it's the right thing to do.

That type of decision may not be favored by your peers but it's still the right thing. You are not here to judge people; you are here to heal them. You saving that individuals life could be the one thing that turns his life around to be a better person maybe even turn his life towards God.

Sometimes you're going to be in situations where there is no one there to make those hard decisions. So, the only one left to make that decision, is you. Always seek Gods advice. But the best rule of thumb is to do what's in the best interest of that patient as an individual. You can always get another job but your typically can't bring someone back from the dead.

LEARN FROM YOUR MISTAKES

Pray for us; for we are confident that we have a good conscience, in all things desiring to live honorably. (Hebrews 13:18)

Everyone has made a mistake or two, it happens. Best way to deal with a mistake is to own up to it, learn from it and become a better nurse for it. As nurses we have a tendency to beat ourselves up after we have made an error. If you make a mistake go confess to your boss by being honest and transparent. They will respect and trust you more for reporting it yourself than them finding out later that you tried to hide your mistake by ignoring it happened or by covering it up. Also, by you telling your boss of the mistake it also gives your boss the time for damage control, to try and fix any problems that could have arose from the mistake.

I have made mistakes, yes, I hate to admit it but it's true. I am sharing a couple of my mistakes in hopes you can learn something from them.

As a new nurse almost 25 years ago I had pulled what I thought was a catapres patch from the box it came in, labeled it with date and my initials then proceeded to apply it to the patient only to find out days later that there is 2 parts to a catapres patch system. The 1st part has the medication in it and the 2nd part has no medication, in which is used to cover the medicated part to the skin of the patient to hold it in place. Sad to say I had only applied the Non-medicated cover up piece to the skin of the patient. Thank God no harm came to the patient. I was embarrassed and felt like an idiot, but guaranteed I will never make that mistake again. I learned that if you don't know something, instead of assuming, ask someone how to do it before doing it.

There was another time I made a mistake where I knew I messed up so I grabbed me a blank write up form took it to my boss, as I entered her office I said, "I messed up" and I started to cry while explaining to her what had happened. I was prepared to accept the consequences of my actions. She knew I would never hurt anyone intentionally and I was very remorseful, snot nose and all. I never got that write up or educational opportunity as they called it, thinking it's because my boss knew I had punished myself enough. I went into this profession to heal people not hurt them. I'm sure you're still wondering what I did. Well I did something to cause a patient to fall out of her wheelchair and get an abrasion to her knee. Once again, Thank God that's all she got because it could have had a worse outcome.

BE A RESTORER

God wants you to be like him and that consists of allowing him to work through you in these ways

He heals the broken hearted and builds up their wounds. (Psalm 147:3)

Therefore, strengthen the hands which hang down, and the feeble knees, and make straight paths for your feet, so that what is lame may not be dislocated, but rather be healed. (Hebrews 12:12)

Then in Jeremiah 30:17 God says he will restore health and heal wounds of the people but he needs you to allow him to work through you. These sick people have a need and you were given a servant's heart to meet those needs.

The Lord will strengthen him on his bed of illness; you will sustain him on his sickbed (Psalm 41:3)

GIVE THEM A SENSE OF PEACE

A soft answer turns away wrath, but a harsh word stirs up anger. (Proverbs 15:1)

When you enter a patients' room, greet the patient gently and kindly.

Watch your tone of voice you use with your patients. Don't bring your problems from home to work and don't bring your stress of work to your patients. It's your responsibility to release peace at work. You do that by partnering with God to release what he says into the atmosphere. By doing this you will provide your patients with an environment that demonstrates compassion and peace; in which will help decrease the patients stress level, pain, healing time and even help decrease negative behaviors of the patients.

Blessed are the peacemakers, for they shall be called sons of God (Matthew 5:9)

BE A TEAM PLAYER

We are in this together. We can't do it without each other. Doctors depend on the nurses to be their eyes and ears and nurses depend on the techs or aides to be their eyes and ears. We need them to help us so we can do our jobs efficiently and effectively. So, treat them with respect, along with other interdisciplinary team members. We are all a work in progress, working towards the same goal.

Apostle Paul speaks on behalf of Jesus asking the people (us) to be team players

Behold how good and how pleasant it is for brethren to dwell together in unity! (Psalm 133:1)

Now I plead with you, brethren, by the name of our Lord Jesus Christ, that you all speak the same thing, and that there be no divisions among you, but that you be perfectly joined together in the same mind and in the same judgement. (1 Corinthians 1:10)

In other words, he wants us to work together as a team, while God is working through us towards one goal; which is to care for and heal the sick, broken and diseased.

"Again, I say to you that if two of you agree on earth concerning anything that they ask, it will be done for them

by My Father in heaven. "For where two or three are gathered together in My name, I am there in the midst of them" (Matthew 18:19-20)

You can't go wrong as a nurse if you do it Gods way and live by these words mentioned in the Bible in Galatians 5:22-23. To be filled with the Fruits of the Spirit you will show love, you will be joyful, you will be their peace, you will be kind, you will be gentle, you will show patience in spite of troubles especially to those caused by other people, and to have faith that it will all work out for good and having self-control in word and actions. Doing it this way and you will inherit the kingdom.

At the end of the day be thankful for his wisdom, guidance and protection.

Let us come before his presence with thanksgiving; Let us shout joyfully to him with psalms. For the Lord is the great God. And the great King above all gods. (Psalm 95:2-3)

PATRICIA DIANE WRIGHT

Founder of Way 2 Wright Living, Licensed Practical Nurse, Certified Christian Life Coach, lives in Grand Rapids, Michigan, and has 2 adult children and 3 grandchildren.

"Together we are going to heal the world one person at a time."